children

Learn

About the Book

In this first report to young Americans on independent Kenya, the author takes us to a country where seven million Africans, two hundred thousand Asians and sixty-five thousand Europeans are attempting to solve their problems. These problems arise from conflicts among themselves as well as from the needs of a land where schools and schoolteachers, hospitals and doctors — and most of all, money — are too scarce.

We visit the "White Highlands" — one of the most disputed areas in all Africa; we meet leaders such as the youthful Tom Mboya, much traveled in the United States, and senior statesman Jomo Kenyatta. We learn that more than thirty different tribes call Kenya home, and we join some of them, such as the wandering Masai carrying the spears and shields they use in cattle disputes with the Kamba tribe. We discover how the government protects its wild animals and we stay up all one night to watch them in a forest preserve.

In contrast with country life is our visit to the new nation's capital, Nairobi, a city of "gleaming metals, glass and colorful ceramic tiles and stone." We move swiftly with the traffic along the city's broad streets and choose from international menus in modern hotels and restaurants.

Finally looking to the future, we speculate whether Kenyans will learn to get along together. We decide to watch for the answers in our newspapers back home.

About the Illustrator

World War II P-47 pilot DON LAMBO got his art training at Pratt Institute, his interest in children's books from his two boys and two girls. Known as an illustrator and advertising artist, he is also a woodworking and photography expert. Personal photographs taken round-the-world are included in the extensive resources from which he has illustrated 14 *Getting to Knows*.

About the Author

Born in Lowell, Massachusetts, educated at Newtown High School and at Columbia University in New York, LEONARD INGALLS, until recently the *New York Times* correspondent in East, Central and South Africa, has since boyhood done everything there is to do in putting out a newspaper, from setting type to writing stories. His father owned a chain of Long Island newspapers.

His own career started with United Press International, took him to the *Herald Tribune* for ten years and then to the *Times*, which he has served as correspondent in London as well as Africa. He is now living in New York.

About the Getting to Know Series

This round-the-world series not only covers everyday life in many countries and regions and includes their geography and history — it also highlights *what's new today*. The series offers timely — and often first — reports on the birth of new nations in Africa and Asia, the splitting of ancient nations like China, the let's-get-together movement of members of Europe's and Latin America's Common Markets, and the struggles of two thirds of the world to attain the good life possessed by the other third. *To keep each book up to date in these fast-changing times, it is revised with every new printing.*

Specific countries in the *Getting to Know* series are determined by a survey of curriculum specialists in the fifty states. Made every two years, the survey is used to relate GTK subject matter to classroom needs. To insure intimacy as well as immediacy, authors are chosen first of all for the quality of their personal experience with the subject matter. All *Getting to Knows* are also checked by experts prior to publication.

ILLUSTRATED BY
DON LAMBO

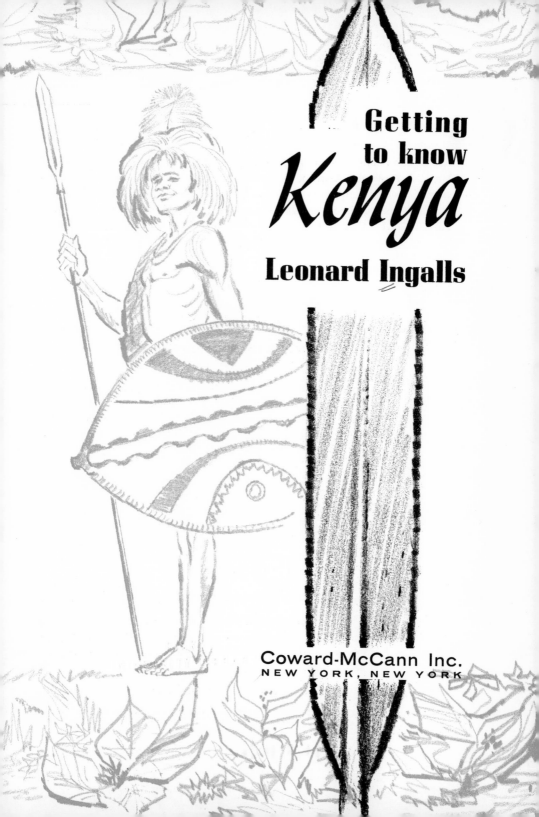

Getting
to know
Kenya
Leonard Ingalls

Coward-McCann Inc.
NEW YORK, NEW YORK

Author and publisher wish to acknowledge with appreciation the cooperation of Mr. C. A. Axworthy, Assistant to the Colonial Attaché, British Embassy, who reviewed this manuscript prior to publication and made many valuable suggestions. Illustrator and publisher are indebted also to Mr. John Gannon of the East Africa Tourist Travel Association for supplying a wealth of material for illustrative purposes.

Also by Leonard Ingalls:

GETTING TO KNOW SOUTH AFRICA

08-012

Fourth Impression

© 1963 BY COWARD-MCCANN, INC.

Library of Congress catalog card number: 63-7743

Editor of this series: Sabra Holbrook

MANUFACTURED IN THE UNITED STATES OF AMERICA

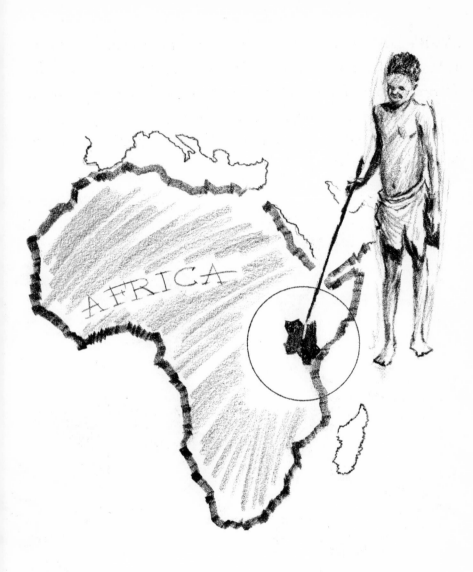

EVERY DAY, travelers board the train at the Indian Ocean port of Mombasa on the east coast of Africa to make the journey to the interior of the continent. Turbaned Arabs, Africans with round embroidered hats, Asian women wearing graceful saris, Europeans in suits, shirts and shorts, all hurry to the station, much as people do all over the world.

Some carry their belongings in shiny leather cases; some bundle their possessions into blankets or sacks. Everybody is in a rush. There is a last-minute jam at the stands selling sandwiches and fruit, newspapers and magazines. Children tug at their mothers' skirts, begging for sweets. The lines in front of the ticket windows grow impatient, but somehow, when the gong sounds and the whistle blows and it's time for the train to depart, everybody manages to be aboard.

The land the travelers will cross is Kenya. With some of its neighbors, Uganda to the west and Tanzania to the south, Kenya is part of a section of the continent that was called British East Africa in the days when England ruled all of these countries. Kenya's other neighbors are Ethiopia to the north and Somalia to the east. In the northwest, it shares a tiny bit of border with Sudan.

Kenya isn't a big country — it's about the size of the two Dakotas and Nebraska put together — but the railroad that starts at Mombasa helped it become an important country in East Africa. This railroad links the markets and producers of the interior with the coast. It connects the Indian Ocean with the very heart of Africa, 1,000 miles away in the former Belgian Congo. We'll ride partway over this famous route after we've explored the port of Mombasa where it starts and meet the people who will be our fellow passengers.

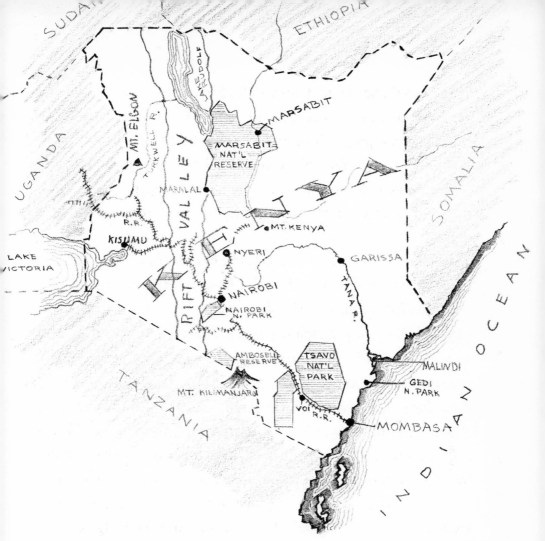

On the streets of Mombasa you meet Africans, Arabs, Asians and
Europeans. They make up Kenya's population of a little more than
7,000,000. The Asians were brought from India by the British to
help build the railroad. In Africa, people from India prefer to be
called Asians, so everybody complies with their wish.

You would be counted among the Europeans, even though you are an American. European is the term Africans generally use to describe white people. The reason is that Europeans were the first and until recently the only white-skinned people the majority of Africans knew. Most of the Europeans in Kenya are British, since the country was a British colony for nearly three quarters of a century.

The Arabs, who today live all along the coastline, were the first men to come to this part of Africa from other lands. It was they who founded the port of Mombasa. Many still dress as their ancestors did in long, flowing white robes, with handsome turbans wound around their heads. Some carry curved daggers in leather scabbards, encrusted with silverwork and jewels. Once the Arabs really used these daggers. In Swahili, an African language with a mixture of Arabic and English words, Mombasa means "island of war." Long ago, the city was on a small island which was the scene of bitter battles. Nowadays glittering Arab daggers are just for decoration.

The city has grown to occupy the mainland too, but its old Arab section is at the north end of the island. After crossing to it by bridge, causeway or ferry, you stroll through narrow alleyways where coffee vendors and carpet dealers keep their shops. You pass buildings that are as old as the city itself. Their thick, white walls have many openings, partly concealed by grillwork. The ceilings are very high. This is a sensible way to build if you want to stay

MOMBASA

cool. Mombasa is very near the equator — and it's hot! Luckily, it's also a place of tall, shady palm trees and, along the mainland, beautiful white sandy beaches. When it's 98° and damp at the same time — as it's often apt to be along Kenya's coast — a swim is very welcome.

At the southern end of the island, a bustling harbor fairly shimmers with heat. The bodies of African dock workers glisten with sweat as they load and unload cargo. Often they sing to make the work go faster. They fill and empty the holds of great steel ships from all over the world.

By comparison with these big ships, the wooden vessels of the Arabs look as tiny as toys. They anchor mostly near the old section in Dhow Harbor. The harbor takes its name from the name of the Arab boats — dhows.

The white-sailed dhows are just like the ones Arabs used when they first came to Africa in the seventh century. The great sails have four sides, with no side the same length as another. Down from Persia and Arabia, Arab adventurers sailed with the trade winds. During certain seasons of the year, these winds blow from the north. Then they shift and blow from the south.

DHOW

The Arabs came down with the north winds and sailed home with the south ones. They loaded their dhows with ivory and gold — and slaves. Between the shift of the winds, they raided African villages in the interior, kidnapped the villagers and shipped them off to be sold into slavery. After 1842 they had to smuggle out their cargo of human flesh. The British Navy was by then patrolling the coast with an antislavery squadron and the Arabs had to choose dark nights to slip past the patrol. Later, when the British took over the area, they were able to put a complete stop to the brutal trade.

Today the dhows still sail back and forth to the Middle East, but their cargo is quite different. They are laden with salt and sisal, which is used to make rope; with poles from mangrove trees and dried coconut from the coconut palms. These and other products from inside Africa come to them via the railroad.

Though the Arabs were the first from other lands to come to this coast, the first from Europe were the Portuguese. In 1498 the Portuguese explorer Vasco da Gama sailed around the Cape of Good Hope at the southern tip of Africa. On the way, he landed at Malindi, another port founded by Arabs and now a popular vacation spot, just a little north of Mombasa.

Thereafter, Mombasa truly became an island of war. The whole coast was one long battlefield. Both Arabs and Portuguese wanted to control it. For a little over 200 years, the Portuguese were on top, but finally the Arabs drove them away.

Then around 1850, explorers from England began to come. They were searching for the source of the River Nile. Finally, after 12 years, they found it in Lake Victoria, which forms part of the western boundary of Kenya.

After the explorers came the traders and after the traders, the settlers. The British East Africa Company, a trading group, had established an inland colony by 1895, but the colony was very difficult to reach. Safaris, the Swahili word for journeys, had to be made on foot or, at best, on horseback. Supplies were carried on the heads or backs of African porters. The trek inland was long and slow. It led through territory where Arabs were still kidnapping Africans and African tribes were fighting each other.

The British wanted to open up the country for trade and farming and they wanted to put a stop to slavery and fighting. To do all these things, it was necessary to be able to travel about. So they decided to start the railroad from Mombasa.

By 1901, the rails reached over 800 miles to the shores of Lake Victoria. By 1926, they reached Kampala, the capital of Uganda, and by 1956 the railroad was extended almost to Uganda's western border. From there trucks complete the link with the Congo.

Now that you have seen the port of Mombasa, you are ready for your train trip and you make your way through the waiting crowd at the station. You will travel to Lake Victoria, a one-day journey. For passengers going as far as Kampala, it's a two-day trip. The passengers will travel in different ways. First-class passengers will ride in stainless-steel cars. They will have compartments for two, where beds are prepared for them to sleep in at night. Those who can't afford first class will ride in wooden cars and sit up all night.

On the trip every stop is an event. People gather at the stations to see the train pull in. Some sell fruit to the passengers, some put on dances. Sometimes an old man with a drum will sing rhythmic folk songs. Some of them he makes up as he goes along. He sings about the train and the weather and about adventures of the past. You throw him a few coins to show your appreciation. As the train pulls out he picks them up and counts them.

Leaving the coast, the train crosses the great plateau of East Africa. The land is flat and monotonous, but keep your eyes open and you won't be bored. Large numbers of Kenya's wild creatures make their homes on this plain and you are likely to see a zebra or a giraffe at any moment, or possibly a mother ostrich with her brood of young.

Beyond the plain, the country rises toward mountains. You notice that the air is cooler now and remains cool as the train crosses some of the highlands nestled between Kenya's two tallest mountains, the dead volcanoes of Mount Kenya and Mount Elgon. Mount Kenya is 17,000 feet high and Mount Elgon is 14,000 feet.

Through the train window you see well-watered valleys with rich vegetation springing from the deep, fertile soil. This is ideal farming country.

Not so the northern section of the country, a fellow passenger

MT. KENYA

tells you. There, it's hot and dry, almost a desert. In some parts of it, there's no rain for years at a time. Here in the lush highlands, plentiful rain usually waters the land between April and June and again between October and December.

When you leave the train at Kisumu, you are on the shores of the second largest lake in the world. Dotted with islands, the light blue waters of Lake Victoria stretch over nearly 27,000 square miles. As you arrive a fleet of African fishermen is setting sail across its broad expanse. They use long poles to shove their striped boats away from shore.

Like these fishermen, and the dock workers you saw back in Mombasa, Africans have always done most of the hard physical labor in Kenya. The better jobs in government and business have generally been held by Kenya's 5,000 Europeans. The 180,000 Asians have done well for themselves, too, as traders, shopkeepers, carpenters, mechanics, doctors and lawyers.

FISHING BOATS ON
LAKE VICTORIA

Some of Kenya's 39,000 Arabs are also prosperous merchants and traders, but many are poor. They are not so poor, however, as the Africans. At the very bottom of the job ladder are the 6,900,000 Africans who are the majority of the country's people. They are only just beginning their upward climb. Although they are being paid more for their work than they used to be, few of them earn over 100 shillings a month. That would be about $14 in American money.

To understand this situation, you need to remember that only 75 years ago, when the British first came to Kenya, few, if any, Africans there had ever heard of mechanics or merchants, doctors or lawyers. The warring tribes had no notion of a central government. All these modern ways of doing things came with the British.

Remarkably, the Africans, confronted with a kind of progress utterly strange to them, were quickly able to recognize and reach for its values. It had taken Europe some 2,000 years to make this progress!

Of course, the tribes had their own ways of organizing society, with rules which were, in some cases, even older than those the British brought. But the rules didn't tell the people such important things as how to prevent or cure disease, and many died unnecessarily. There was no rule that guaranteed enough to eat, and many starved. There was no chance for education as we know it. There was no contact with the world beyond the tribal homeland and therefore no way of knowing how to trade and work with others to achieve a common good.

That Africans haven't mastered the means of doing *all* these things in a mere 75 years isn't so very surprising, is it? Lots of people might not even try. They might just be content with their old-fashioned ways. The fact that these skills take time to acquire is one of the reasons Africans have been at the bottom of the modern job ladder for what seems to them so very long, even though history might judge the period as a very short one.

But like most people, Africans are more interested in their lot today than in what history will say tomorrow. And so their low rung on the job ladder has naturally caused bad feelings among them toward the other groups. The Africans are in an understandable hurry to have jobs that pay *them* enough to let them vacation in Malindi and ride in the steel cars with the comfortable beds. They are ambitious to live and work and play as the others do — *now*. They are eager for the education that will help them climb the job ladder. Although today more of them go to school for longer periods, 80 percent of the grown-ups still can't read or write.

Education is also necessary for self-goverment. Governing themselves has been another big goal of Africans in Kenya, as it has been everywhere on the continent, especially in recent years. After many conferences in London between 1960 and 1962, African leaders of Kenya won several important agreements. It was agreed that Kenya should have full self-government under the British in 1963 and independence from the British soon thereafter. It was also agreed that in the meantime, Africans, the majority of the population, should have a majority in the country's Legislative Council. A new constitution was created for the country and the task of working out its details was given to Africans representing Kenya's principal political parties.

One of the leaders in this struggle for independence was Jomo Kenyatta. By the time the agreements were won, he had fought a long time and spent many years in jail because the British courts found him guilty of directing a terrible revolutionary movement known as Mau Mau.

Mr. Kenyatta was born a member of the Kikuyu tribe, the largest in Kenya. As you probably know from watching television reports on Africa, the continent contains not only many different peoples, but an even larger number of different tribes. In Kenya alone, there are more than 30. National boundaries often mean little to African tribes. The boundaries were drawn by Europeans, not Africans, and were sometimes drawn in such a way that a tribe spread across several nations. Consequently, loyalty to the tribe frequently comes before loyalty to a nation. Tribal allegiance is so strong that it even determines which political party a voter will join. In politics, as in private life, each tribe guards with great zeal what it considers to be its special rights. The tribes have their own special languages, too, but fortunately in Kenya most of them also understand Swahili.

The home of Mr. Kenyatta's tribe, the Kikuyu, is on the slopes of Mount Kenya. The Kikuyu believe the mountain was the birthplace of their tribal founders, and as such, they worship it. They are very fond of secret societies and take oaths as members of these groups to support tribal aims. Mau Mau was such a secret society.

One of the main aims of the Mau Mau was to drive Europeans from Kenya and to set up an African government. After Mr. Kenyatta was put in jail in 1952, the Mau Mau society put Kenya through four years of terror in which many were killed and injured. Some of the victims were Europeans, but most were Africans.

KIKUYU WOMAN

LUO TRIBESMAN

You see, not all the Kikuyu tribe sympathized with the use of violence by the Mau Mau members. They believed that Africans should win their freedom by peaceful means. Some of them helped the British government of Kenya form a home guard to protect people from the terrorists. Then the Mau Mau attacked these Africans and killed many of them and their families.

While the rebellion was at its peak and Mr. Kenyatta was in jail, another important political leader came onto the scene. His name was Tom Mboya, and he was a young man in his mid-twenties. He belonged to the Luo tribe, the second largest in the country. Its members came from the shores of Lake Victoria. The fishermen you watched there were Luo people.

23

While in his twenties, Tom Mboya got a job in Nairobi, the country's capital, as Sanitary Inspector in the health department. On his inspections, he saw a great deal of poverty and disease. He saw people living in shabby huts with few chances to improve their lives. The uniform he wore in his job, the bicycle he rode, became to him the symbols of the lowly position, with no way out, to which he believed Africans were being confined. He grew to resent the uniform and the bike. He decided to do something for himself and his people.

So he started organizing labor unions. A labor union is an organization through which workers bargain with their bosses about wages and working conditions. By 1953, Mboya had become General Secretary of the Kenya Federation of Labor, and in 1955, when he was only twenty-five years old, he won national fame by settling a strike of dock workers in Mombasa. He did it by persuading the workers to submit their argument to an arbitration committee — an impartial group. The result was that the workers got a one-third increase in pay.

During all this time, Mr. Mboya had wanted to organize a political party, but while the Mau Mau rebellion was raging he couldn't, because political parties weren't permitted until it ended. The army finally put a stop to Mau Mau terror in 1958 and in 1960 young Tom Mboya helped found KANU, the Kenya African National Union. 1960 was also the year, you will remember, when the British had begun the conferences looking toward Kenya's independence. The formation of political parties became a necessary step toward self-rule.

KANU became the largest political party in the country. Not only the Luo and Kikuyu joined it, but also the third largest tribe, the Kamba.

KAMBA DANCER

In 1961 Mr. Kenyatta was set free by the British and became the president of KANU. In 1962, he was appointed one of the chief ministers of the government. To his people he became known as their greatest leader, and Tom Mboya, who was secretary of the party, became known as their young leader. At political meetings, these leaders would often wear their tribal costumes, each man carrying a fly whisk made of a zebra's tail, or the hair of some other coarse-furred animal. Such whisks are African symbols of authority.

Not everyone in Kenya was satisfied with the Kenyatta-Mboya party. In the beginning, some feared that the big tribes who belonged to it, Luo and Kamba and especially the Kikuyu, might try to rule the country all by themselves. And so another party, supported by the smaller tribes, KADU, the Kenya African Democratic Union, had been started at the same time as KANU. Ronald Ngala, of the Giriama tribe, became its president.

Mr. Ngala was a former schoolteacher who came from north of Mombasa. A thoughtful man, he liked to sit smoking a pipe as he developed his ideas. Under his leadership, KADU succeeded in strengthening the bill of rights in the new constitution so that it contained safeguards to protect smaller tribes against the bigger ones.

On December 12, 1963, Kenya obtained *uhuru*, Swahili for freedom-and-independence. Mr. Ngala named his tenth child Uhuru and he and his KADU followers joined KANU to give the new country unity. It became a republic with Mr. Kenyatta as President and Tom Mboya as Minister of Economic Planning and Development. *Harambee*, Swahili for "work together," was the country's motto.

You would enjoy attending a Kenyan political meeting. They are often colorful occasions. If you have ever seen American political conventions on television, you have noticed delegates dressed up in fancy hats carrying banners and snake-dancing in the aisles. Africans do much the same thing in their own way. In addi-

tion to beaded caps and fly whisks, the leaders sometimes wear flowing garments decorated with the skins of long-haired colobus monkeys. Others use lion or leopard skins. Drums beat as some of the
men and women in tribal dress dance to entertain the crowds before
the speeches start.

Tribal ways and loyalties play such an important part in life in Kenya that you will want to get to know more of them. You haven't yet met the Masai, those great warriors of the past who are still regarded as a fierce and proud people. They live much the same way today as they have for hundreds of years. Dressed in their rust-colored blankets, their arms glittering with metal bracelets and their necks looped with shining beads, they wander over the plains of Kenya.

MASAI PEOPLE

They are nomads, driving their cattle before them. They prize their herds highly. Although there are only about 600,000 Masai, they own about 750,000 head of cattle. The men carry long spears and shields and are ready to fight any man or beast that tries to harm or steal their herds. They frequently get into cattle feuds with the Kamba tribe. The Masai believe that the more cattle they have, the richer they are. Consequently, they never kill the cattle for food. Instead, they take blood and milk from them and mix these together to make a basic food.

The government is trying to help the Masai realize that they will have better cattle if they keep fewer of them. Although the plains where the tribe wanders are big — some 15,000 square miles — much of the land is dry and the cattle overgraze the lush parts around watering points. The overgrazing reduces the good land still more when already there isn't enough to feed the cattle properly.

The Masai are one group of many cattle lovers in Kenya. Like the Masai, the others are often reluctant to slaughter their herds even though they like meat. They can't get much wild game, since strict laws protect it. Consequently, many tribespeople live mainly on a diet of such plain but plentiful foods as beans and maize, which is a kind of corn.

Among the other famous cattle people are the Turkana. They live in the northwest of Kenya in the Rift Valley. This 40-mile-wide valley lies from 2,000 to 3,000 feet below the surrounding countryside. It's part of a great depression in the earth that begins in the Dead Sea and the Jordan River, continues through the Red Sea into Ethiopia, then down through Kenya, Tanzania and Mozambique into the Indian Ocean. The Rift was probably created thousands of years ago by some tremendous earthquake. Kenya's Lake Rudolf and other lakes in East Africa were also formed by it.

The Turkana migrated to this valley from Ethiopia. Long ago, legends say, a young man who was searching for a lost ox wandered there. He didn't find the ox but he met a beautiful young woman

TURKANA
POLICEMAN

of his own tribe who had also wandered from home. Around them, they saw a rich, green country, empty of people, where wild fruits and berries and all kinds of good things grew in abundance. The young pair found the valley so enchanting that when they returned to their homeland, they encouraged other young men and women to come and settle there with them. And that was how the Turkana came to Kenya.

Today Turkana believe that some animals are in touch with the souls of the tribe's ancestors. Each family has a few such special animals which are supposed to be able to persuade the ancestors to help the family prosper. These bringers-of-blessings are worshiped with songs of praise.

A boy who is about to become a man will certainly ask a family animal to secure his ancestors' blessings. At the age of about thirteen, a boy is initiated into manhood by taking a test of courage. The test requires that he kill an angry bull with his spear. As the boy pits his skill against the strength of the bull, the men of the tribe look on. For the occasion they put on their most elaborate ornaments. Ropes of beads encircle their necks like collars reaching almost up to their chins. Shining coils of metal spiral around their upper arms. They wear long fancy headdresses made of giraffe hair. Attached to each man's lower lip is a carved ball of ivory, matched by another ivory ball in the center of his necklace.

The various tribes of Kenya have many festivities you would

enjoy watching. The Embu perform a dance on stilts. The dancers are dressed in scary black cloaks and wear white masks made of animal skins. The Kamba, who are known as Kenya's most athletic tribe, do a dance which features double somersaults.

RINDA (SKIRT)

There is interesting variety in tribal fashions, too. The women of Mr. Ngala's Giriama wear beautiful pleated white skirts, something like a short tennis skirt. It takes 40 yards of white cotton to make a *rinda*, which is the Giriama name for this creation. Dancers of Mr. Kenyatta's Kikuyu paint crescents, crosses and other symbols on their faces. The symbols are drawn in dotted white lines which glisten like pearls against their dark skin. The men of Mr. Mboya's Luo like to wear the horns of wild beasts in their hair when they are dressed up.

35

The Luo used to be very fierce fighters. They fought like the Romans in a tight-knit phalanx, or square, of men. The outer rows on all four sides looked like walls of shields. Their weapons were spears, but instead of throwing them, they plunged them into their enemies. Today the Luo are more peaceful.

The Giriama are also a peaceful tribe, though they are famous for making a deadly poison which they sell to other tribes. However, it's used mostly to kill animals. The Giriama raised cattle until the Masai stole all their herds. Now they are farmers.

Cattle raising or farming is the main occupation of all the tribes. Some of the farmers till the soil with only a little hand hoe. Others have learned to use a plow drawn by oxen. Those who work on large farms owned by Europeans have been trained to use tractors and other farm machinery. A few who have learned how efficient these machines are and can afford to buy them, have started to use them on their own farms.

Kenyans earn most of their money by selling farm products to the rest of the world. They are making great efforts to increase the production of coffee, tea and pyrethrum, which are their specialties. Pyrethrum is a pretty white flower that can be crushed to make a powerful chemical for killing insect pests. Sisal is also an important crop.

One of the big problems that hindered progress in farming for a long time was land fragmentation. This was a complicated system

PYRETHRUM MAKING

of dividing up a man's land after he died. He willed it to his children or relatives in pieces. When they died, the pieces were cut up still farther and parceled out to their descendants. The result, after

a few generations, was that a farmer might end up owning many widely separated bits of land. Each was fenced and cultivated.

From an airplane, this arrangement made the countryside look like an enormous patchwork quilt. Farmers had to waste much time going from one patch to another, and they worked so hard to make things grow on little patches that they overtaxed the soil. It had nothing left in it to feed crops, and it became so loose that when the rains came, much of it was washed away.

Government experts went to the people and persuaded them to turn in their pieces of land so that they could be combined. In return for scattered bits, farmers received one large piece. Then they no longer had to travel to cultivate it. The government experts also taught the farmers how to build terraces and to rotate their crops. The rotation helped the earth to keep its goodness and the terraces prevented the soil from washing away.

Land has always been precious in Kenya because two-thirds of the country is semidesert where nothing useful will grow. There hasn't been enough good land to go around. And a large part of the good land, the lush and lovely country between Mount Kenya and Mount Elgon which you glimpsed on your train ride from Mombasa, was set aside for European farmers.

It was called the "White Highlands" and until recently no African farmer was permitted to own land there. Africans could only go there to work for European farm owners. Many of them did.

Some were well treated by their employers, others were not. But discontent grew strong among the well-treated and the ill-treated alike, and also among others who were not in the White Highlands, but who wanted to farm there. They all resented not being able to own any of the land. This resentment was part of what started the Mau Mau uprising.

European farmers built beautiful homes in the White Highlands, where the green hills and meadows reminded them of England. From abroad they brought fine cattle to the lush pastures. Many of them lived and farmed there for several generations and came to love the land. They didn't want to give it up to Africans. At the same time, many of them had more than they could use. There were tracts that weren't being farmed at all. The Africans looked at these tracts and it didn't seem right to them that there should be a law preventing them from using some of this land.

They held political meetings to talk against restricting land ownership in the Highlands to the Europeans. They argued also in the Legislative Council. Finally, the government changed the regulations and said that anybody could own land in the Highlands. It agreed to buy from Europeans more than a million acres so that landless Africans could settle there. The government purchase permitted European farmers who didn't want to stay in Kenya to get back some of the money they had invested in their farms and go home.

There were a number of European farmers who did just that. They said they didn't want to live with African neighbors, and they didn't want to live under an independent African government. Other farmers said they would stay a while and wait and see what would happen.

Still others worked with the Africans to help them learn to farm, to get an education and to become ready to govern themselves. The Europeans who worked with Africans were not many, but they tried to do something big. They tried hard to build in Kenya a society in which people of all races and backgrounds would be treated fairly. They started multiracial clubs. They helped Africans form political parties and labor unions. They advised them on family problems. They became friends.

Perhaps most important of all, they worked to find scholarships for young people. Most African parents are eager to have their children go to school. They are especially eager for their sons to be educated. Some tribes used to believe that girls didn't need an education. What would they use it for? Women were supposed only to have children, take care of them and help out in the fields. But as more boys were educated, they began to have a hard time finding wives with whom they could be happy. The girls didn't know as much as they did. So now that the men are realizing it is just as necessary for girls to go to school as for boys, the number of girls in classrooms is increasing.

In towns and cities of Kenya, most of the classrooms are much like yours. They are light and airy with many windows. In the country, schools may be built just as the people's homes are: of mud and sticks and grass. The people handle grass as a building material in a very clever way. They use a great many layers, clipping them in such a fashion that they get a tough covering that keeps out rain and wind. Sometimes a whole house may be made of grass layers on a framework of wood. Most houses are round with a hole in the center of the roof to let out the smoke of the cooking fire. They look something like beehives. Some of the schools are just as simply built.

Other schools may have no shelter at all, except for a shady tree. The children sit under it, on the ground, and the teacher sits on a stool or stands up in front of them. She reads to the pupils or tells them about the lesson. The amount they learn depends on how much she knows. There aren't yet enough trained teachers to tell the children all they would like to find out.

The lack of teachers and of school buildings is one of the reasons why most African children in Kenya never get to high school. A majority of them now go to elementary school, which lasts for six or eight years — but that's all. Since so few go to high school, few also go to college. Those who do, go mainly to England and the United States. Some go to India and a few to the Soviet Union.

Each year the school children have three long vacations. There's one at Christmastime and one around Easter. The longest comes in

August and lasts into September. In June and July, school is open. The schedule is like the one in England. As in England, the children call the school grades "forms."

OPEN AIR SCHOOL

Having been a British colony, Kenya follows many British practices, such as the big parade of troops, and the firing of cannons that celebrates the birthday of the Queen of England. Crowds gather to watch and listen to the band music. The African troops are smartly dressed and they march with great dignity and precision.

Also from England come the games of Rugby football and cricket, both extremely popular with Africans. In Rugby the ball may be kicked, carried or thrown backwards. The players tackle each other as hard as in American football, but they wear no helmets or protective suits — just shorts and jerseys.

Cricket is something like baseball. It's played by two teams of eleven men each. The team uses bats and balls and makes runs. The game is a lot more complicated than baseball, however. It can take as long as two days to complete two innings.

Boys like to play soccer in the schoolyard. Both boys and girls play many games with a stick and ball. Sometimes they make them up. They like to chase each other through the forest and make believe they are hunting wild animals. In one remote part of Kenya, some children invented a game with a real wild animal, a rhinoceros. They called their game "spear-on, spear-off." A boy must creep up to a sleeping rhinoceros and place a spear on his back. The next boy must remove the spear without waking the rhinoceros.

Many of the holidays children enjoy are connected with their religions. Asian boys and girls look forward to Divali, a festival of

lights that marks the triumph of good over evil. Little candles or lighted lamps appear on window ledges. Fireworks also play a big part in this festival. Sometimes so many are exploded all at once, they sound as though a battle were being fought. Divali is a festival of the Hindu religion which Asians brought with them from India. Hindus believe that God takes many forms and they worship Him in all of them.

The Arabs in Kenya are Moslems. One of their holidays comes at the end of Ramadan. It's a big feast at the end of a long fast. During Ramadan, which is the ninth month in the Moslem calendar, Moslems fast and pray. Then, when the month is over, families kill a goat or sheep and eat to their hearts' content. Afterward, they visit friends and there are cakes and candies and other goodies for all the children.

Moslems worship one God, Allah. They believe that Allah's greatest prophet was a man named Mohammed. They also believe that Jesus and Abraham were great prophets.

There are about 1,300,000 Christians in Kenya, including Europeans and Africans. They celebrate Christmas and Easter much as Christians do everywhere. Other Africans, as you have seen, worship things in nature, such as mountains and animals. They are called animists. Some believe that there are both good and evil spirits in nature. They also believe that witch doctors can control these spirits with magic.

Still other Africans combine Christianity with animist beliefs and tribal practices. On Sunday afternoons, you see these worshipers dressed in white robes, holding services to the beat of drums. The leaders of these groups call themselves Messiahs.

For all children of Kenya who live in the country, it's a holiday whenever they can visit the cities. Sometimes their teachers take them to Nairobi, the capital. You would enjoy taking the trip with them. You climb into a bus crowded with passengers and maybe also with goats and chickens. The passengers are allowed to carry all kinds of things with them, and they do — including livestock. The roof of the bus is piled up with bicycles. Many of the passengers who get off along the way to town must continue their journey along narrow paths to their villages. The bike is a handy means to get home.

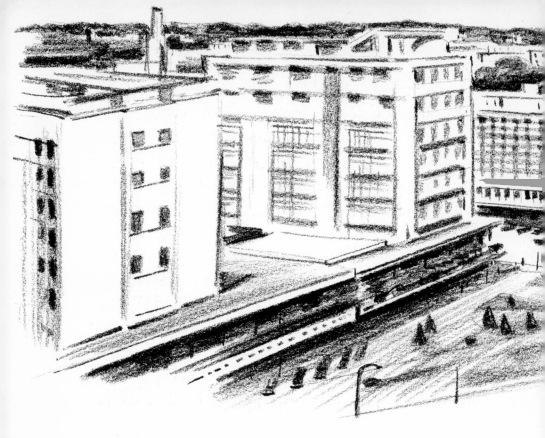

In Nairobi there are many things for you to see. On the main street, Delamere Avenue, is a statue of the man for whom the street is named. Lord Delamere persuaded many of his fellow Englishmen that Kenya was a good place for them to come and settle. The street is lined with new buildings of modern design. They are made of gleaming metals, glass and colorful ceramic tiles and stone.

Traffic moves swiftly along Delamere Avenue and other broad streets. Around you, you hear people speaking English, Swahili and some of the Asian tongues, such as Gujarati, which is the language of people from Gujarat, a province of India.

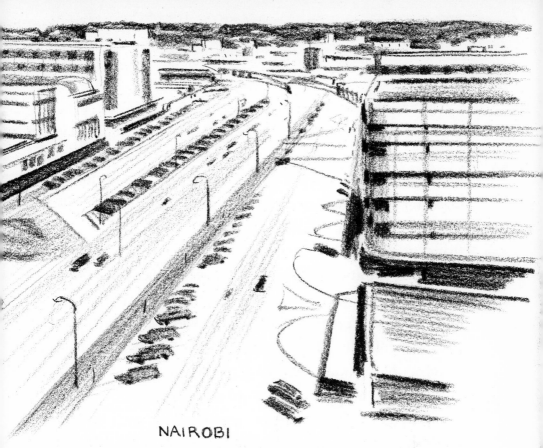

NAIROBI

Look! There's a Masai, wrapped in his blanket and carrying his spear, moving past the man with the beard and turban. The bearded man is a Sikh. He belongs to a Hindu sect whose members are known for being fierce fighters. The two men pass each other and are lost in a crowd of people in Western dress. Some of the men wear slacks and cool, open-necked sport shirts. The women and girls make spots of flashing color with their bright, figured cotton dresses. One mother has tied an orange bandanna around her head. Her little boy wears khaki shorts.

The children with you may beg to go to the movies. They like the films from London and Hollywood. However, the teacher has decided to take the group to the Coryndon Museum. It's a natural history museum, and while you look at the exhibits of stuffed animals and birds, the insects, reptiles and trees, the teacher tells you about the museum's famous curator, Dr. Louis S. B. Leakey. A British scientist, Dr. Leakey was born and brought up among the Kikuyu by his missionary parents. He was initiated into manhood along with Kikuyu boys by taking with them a test of courage much like the Turkana's. Tribal boys who are initiated together form a club for life. Thus Coryndon's curator always remained a member of his Kikuyu initiation club. He once said of himself that in many ways he was more Kikuyu than British!

Dr. Leakey's discoveries have contributed a great deal to our knowledge of the origins of mankind. Forty miles east of Lake Victoria, he found the remains of a two-legged, manlike creature that scientists believe lived 14 million years ago. He also unearthed in Kenya the skull of a primitive ape that lived from 25 to 40 million years ago. He dug up bones of a giraffe that was only the size of a donkey and of an elephant no larger than a cow. He found forms of hippopotamus and rhinoceros that no longer exist. From these strange and ancient bones and skeletons of Kenya and neighboring Tanganyika, scientists are developing new ideas about the growth of life on earth.

If you were visiting Nairobi as a tourist, rather than with school children, you wouldn't want to miss seeing an exhibition of tribal dancing at the African Stadium. The exhibitions are put on by the very best dancers of Kenya's many tribes. All the dances have meanings. Some celebrate historic battles; some celebrate family affairs, such as weddings. All are centuries old. Costumed in feathers, cloth and animal skins, the performers are a thrilling sight as they leap wildly in the air or shuffle rhythmically to the urgent throbbing of the drums.

After the performance, you might return to your modern hotel. For dinner, you could choose from restaurants that serve food from many countries: France, Italy, China, England, India and lands of the Middle East. From India comes a dish that will make you reach for water in a hurry if you take too big a mouthful. It's curry —

hotly spiced meat or rice or vegetables or all three together. Curry is popular with both Europeans and Africans. Another dish which Africans consider a delicacy is fried grasshoppers. At night, when the insects cluster around the streetlights, you'll see people gathering them.

It's possible that you might see a lion in Nairobi. A few years ago a lion prowled through the main streets. The poor beast was so frightened by the people and the traffic that it went berserk and had to be destroyed.

Of course, wild animals don't usually come into the city, but they sometimes do come very close to the big international airport just outside it. The Royal Nairobi Park, a game preserve, is near the airport and when there hasn't been any rain for a long time, and the animals' normal feeding places have dried up, zebras and antelope may come to graze the green grass at the side of the road leading to the airfield. If your plane flies low, taking off or landing, you may see some startled animals galloping for cover.

There are other larger game preserves where you can see hundreds of animals eat — Marsabit in the north and Tsavo and Amboseli near the Tanzanian border. Tsavo covers 8,000 square miles. It's one of the world's largest national parks. All together Kenya has nine national parks and reserves.

Perhaps the most unusual spot from which to watch wild animals is Treetops, about 50 miles from Mount Kenya. Treetops is a hotel that rests in the tops of several trees. The original Treetop was just a small house in one great tree. When it was destroyed in the Mau Mau uprising, the new Treetops was built. On its two floors, it can take care of twenty guests.

Imagine you are on your way to Treetops. You have to walk the last mile through the jungle. Along the trail you see ladders leaning against some of the trees. They are there so that you can scramble up them if wild animals come too close. You needn't worry too much, though; your guide carries a rifle to protect you if beasts should attack.

When you arrive at the hotel, you climb a flight of stairs to reach it. You might think that living in a tree would be like camping out. But no, Treetops has running water and electric lights. You have a fine hot dinner, then sit on the long porch to watch the animals. Below you is a pond where they come to drink. Salt has been put out for them to lick, so as to attract as many as possible. Elephants, buffaloes, hippopotamuses, and eland, which are huge elk weighing over 1,500 pounds, lumber out of the shadowy forest. Tall giraffes crane their necks down to the water. All night long the parade of striped and spotted beasts, of furry creatures big and

small, continues. Who could go to bed? Not you and none of the other guests either. How silly to sleep away this one night in a lifetime. No one could possibly dream anything as exciting as the spectacle from Treetops!

These animals are very important to Kenya. They are a source of money. Each year, the government gives out a limited number of licenses to hunters who want to shoot them. This chance to hunt the big game attracts sportsmen from many foreign lands and they spend large amounts in Kenya.

Some of the tribespeople, however, don't bother about licenses. They catch the animals in wire snares or kill them with poisoned arrows. They especially like to catch elephants because their ivory tusks are so valuable. Killing the wild game without a license is called poaching and those caught doing it are punished.

Hunters hire guides to take them to the places where the animals abound. The guides arrange safaris for people who just want to shoot the animals with cameras as well as for those who want to shoot them with guns. Sometimes a safari is only a few days long, but some may take many weeks or even months. The guides are called "white hunters." They are Europeans who have lived for a long time in Africa and know the bush trails and the animal haunts.

A modern safari can be a very civilized adventure. When you come home to camp at night after a day of hunting from early morning, you head for the portable shower bath. Then you have a

SAFARI

fine meal. Your thirst is slaked by cold drinks, iced in a portable refrigerator that operates on kerosene.

After dinner, there are songs and stories around the campfire, but you are soon sleepy after the long day and the good meal and happy to go to bed on a comfortable air mattress. You are floating off to sleep, when suddenly — what's that?

Sitting up, you hear the lions growl. At first the sound is just a rumble. Then they roar so loud they seem to shake the earth. Falling asleep isn't so easy as you thought it would be. Birds twitter and scream, monkeys chatter and hyenas bark and howl. But you are so tired you finally fall asleep anyway. Only your guide is still awake, keeping in touch with his headquarters by radio. "All is well," he wires. If anything were wrong, a small plane would fly to the camp with help. If someone were injured, the plane would fly him to a hospital in Nairobi.

Radio is an important means of communication all over Kenya. It links many remote parts of the country. Transistor radios are inexpensive and thousands of people own them. The Kenya Broadcasting Service puts on daily programs in Swahili, English and some of the Asian languages. Broadcasts bring news of the world to some of the bush villages as well as to all the towns and cities. In 1962, television, too, came to Kenya. It was one of the first African countries to have it.

News also travels through daily newspapers in both English and Swahili. Weekly newspapers are published in these languages and in some of the Asian tongues. In city bookshops, newspapers and magazines from England and the United States appear along with the latest books.

Radio, television and newspaper stories tell Kenyans not only what is happening in their own country but what happens all over their continent and, indeed, the world. They know that Africans have fewer of the good things of the modern world than people who live in western Europe and North America. The tribal leaders with their zebras' tails, the fishermen of Lake Victoria, the dock workers of Mombasa — they all want these things too.

As you have seen, Kenya, though primitive in many ways, is modern in enough ways to want to become more so. Its people look both backward to the customs and beliefs of their ancestors and forward to taking their place in the world as citizens of an independent nation.

For more than half the twentieth century, association with the British helped Africans of Kenya prepare for independence. The British helped them fight poverty, ignorance and disease. To do this, they have spent since World War II the equivalent of over $45,000,000 from the Colonial Development and Welfare Funds,

56

which the British use to aid their colonies all over the world. Kenya is also now getting generous aid from the United States, the German Federal Republic and the United Nations, of which it is a member.

In the beginning, in the old days, the British helped the Africans in order to help themselves. If the colony was to prosper, they needed healthy people with enough education to be good workers. So they built schools and hospitals. They needed transportation to bring from the interior products which could be sold the world over. So they built the railroad and they built roads.

But as time went on, the British began to help Africans for the benefit of the Africans as well as themselves. Most important of all, they began actively preparing Kenya to join the Commonwealth, an association of former British colonies, now self-governing, who work together for the benefit of all. Kenya is today a member.

Preparing Kenya for self-government, the British showed the people how to do things for themselves. They helped farmers learn how to fight soil erosion, plant disease and insect pests. They taught local officials how to run a fair government through a system known as "localization." Under this system, a Kenyan and a British administrator worked together in a government job until the Kenyan learned from experience how to handle it.

To the new Kenya, the old colonial government has passed on a heritage not only of physical improvements, but of knowledge of how to make them. The African government of Kenya will have to use this knowledge to continue all these efforts.

If the government is to succeed, such things as differences between tribes will have to be forgotten — except, perhaps, in history books. The government will need to persuade the Kikuyu and the Luo, the Masai and the Kamba to work together and stop trying to steal each other's cattle. Big tribes will have to be big enough to give little ones a square deal. Small tribes like the Somali in the north will have to stop talking about forming a separate country of their own. Arabs on the coastal strip will also have to give up the idea of going it alone. Kenya is already small, as modern states go, and fractions of Kenya would be far too small to survive by themselves.

Europeans, Arabs and Asians must get used to living in a country governed by Africans, and the African government must protect the rights of all these groups. Without *umoja*, which is Swahili for unity, uhuru might bring only civil war. Kenya's birthday as a new nation could have been celebrated much earlier if it hadn't been for lack of unity among the people.

Indeed, only a little more than a year after its birthday, the country might have been split apart — if the British, at President Kenyatta's request, hadn't sent soldiers to put down a Kenyan Army rebellion. Singing "Auld Lang Syne," the last British troops had left the country in a blue, white and silver plane, two days before independence. "Your departure," Mr. Kenyatta had said, "has earned the British Army our further good will." Now, in January 1964, Mr. Kenyatta called the British soldiers back to help him put down the mutiny.

Lack of unity raises a question about the future of non-Africans in Kenya. Tom Mboya has said that an African is "anyone who wants to make Africa his home," and Jomo Kenyatta has said that "all will be treated equally, irrespective of race or color." The man he appointed as his Minister of Agriculture is a European.

However, not all Mr. Mboya's and Mr. Kenyatta's fellow citizens are as hospitable as they. Disagreements about the future of non-Africans as well as that of Africans themselves are so deep that nobody can be absolutely sure there will not be trouble.

The leaders of the new country, however, are trying to prevent Kenya from wasting time and energy in squabbles. The country is small and poor and has much to do to meet the people's needs. Lately, the leaders have been holding two kinds of talks, one within Kenya and another with its neighbors.

In Kenya they have been trying to see whether tribal differences would be less troublesome if the country were divided into six regions which tribes of those areas could rule under the central government. Nairobi, the capital, would be a special district, something like Washington, D.C.

With neighboring and newly independent Tanzania and Uganda, which are also small and poor, the leaders have discussed forming an East African Federation. Under British rule these countries for some time shared a common banking, communications and transportation system. If they were to share a common government, they could manage to do more for themselves and do it at less cost. This possibility, however, is a long time off. In June, 1965, Tanzania withdrew partially from the joint system and said she would get out entirely in another year. It seems that Kenya isn't likely to get much cooperation from her Tanzanian neighbor.

Now that you know something about Kenya's past and present, you can guess about its future and watch your newspapers and television to see how good your guesses are. You'll want to make some good wishes, too, for an eager people on an uphill road. They very much want to reach the top, but they find the way up hard, and being in a hurry, they sometimes get out of breath.

Steep as Mount Kenya, the home of the Kikuyu, is the road to nationhood — to the umoja that must strengthen uhuru. But how exciting when you arrive!

HOW TO PRONOUNCE NAMES AND FOREIGN WORDS IN THIS BOOK

Word	Pronunciation	Word	Pronunciation
dhow	dow	Mombasa	Mom-*bah*-sah
		Mount Elgon	*Ell*-gon
Embu	*Em*-boo		
		Nairobi	Neye-*robe*-ee
Giriama	Jeer-ee-*ah*-mah	Ngala, Ronald	En-*gah*-lah
Harambee	Hah-*rahm*-bee		
Kamba	*Kam*-bah	Somali	Soh-*mah*-lee
Kampala	Kam-*pal*-ah	Somalia	Soh-*mahl*-yah
Kenya	Keen-yah	Swahili	Swah-*heel*-ee
Kenyatta, Jomo	Ken-*yah*-tah,		
	Joh-moh	Tanganyika	Tan-gan-*yee*-kah
Kikuyu	Kee-*koo*-you	Turkana	Ter-*kah*-nah
Luo	*Lou*-oh	Uganda	You-*gahn*-dah
		uhuru	oo-*hoo*-roo
Malindi	Mal-*in*-dee	umoja	ooh-*moh*-jah
Mau Mau	Mow Mow		
Masai	Mass-*eye*		
Mboya, Tom	Em-*boy*-yah		

SAY IT IN SWAHILI

English	Swahili	Pronunciation
Hello	Jambo	*jahm*-boh
Good-by	Kwaheri	kwah-*hay*-ree
Please	Tafadhali	tah-fah-*vahl*-ee
Thank you	Ahsante	ah-*sahn*-tee
We are friends.	Tuko rafiki.	*too*-koh rah-*fee*-kee

62

HISTORY

7th Century — Coast settled by Arabs.

1498 — Vasco da Gama lands at Malindi and Portuguese subsequently seize control of coast from Arabs.

1729 — Arabs regain control.

1862 — British explorers discover the source of the Nile in Lake Victoria.

1888 — British traders, from British East Africa Company, arrive on the coast.

1890 — The British establish a protectorate and abolish slavery.

1895 — The British found the first inland colony.

1897 — Lord Delamere and other settlers arrive.

1900 — Kenya-Uganda railroad begun. Indians from Asia imported to help build it.

1926 — Railroad reaches Kampala.

1940 — Italy briefly occupies part of northern Kenya, during World War II.

1952 — Emergency measures taken to suppress Mau-Mau Society rebellion. Jomo Kenyatta imprisoned.

1955 — Land consolidation program started.

1956 — Railroad reaches western Uganda border.

1960 — Political parties, Kenya African National Union and Kenya African Democratic Union, are founded. Africans win right to a majority in the Legislative Council. British announce plan to buy land in the White Highlands to be turned over to Africans.

1961 — Kenyatta freed.

1962 — New constitution drawn. Kenyatta appointed a government minister.

1963 — Kenya became independent. Kenyatta elected President of the new republic.

INDEX

THE GETTING TO KNOW BOOKS

COVER TODAY'S WORLD

Africa

GETTING TO KNOW AFRICA'S FRENCH COMMUNITY
GETTING TO KNOW ALGERIA
GETTING TO KNOW THE CONGO RIVER
GETTING TO KNOW EGYPT
GETTING TO KNOW KENYA
GETTING TO KNOW LIBERIA
GETTING TO KNOW NIGERIA
GETTING TO KNOW THE SAHARA
GETTING TO KNOW SOUTH AFRICA
GETTING TO KNOW RHODESIA,
      ZAMBIA AND MALAWI
GETTING TO KNOW TANZANIA

Arctic

GETTING TO KNOW THE ARCTIC

Asia

GETTING TO KNOW BURMA
GETTING TO KNOW THE CENTRAL HIMALAYAS
GETTING TO KNOW HONG KONG
GETTING TO KNOW INDIA
GETTING TO KNOW JAPAN
GETTING TO KNOW THE NORTHERN HIMALAYAS
GETTING TO KNOW PAKISTAN
GETTING TO KNOW THE RIVER GANGES
GETTING TO KNOW THAILAND
GETTING TO KNOW THE TWO CHINAS
GETTING TO KNOW THE TWO KOREAS
GETTING TO KNOW THE TWO VIETNAMS

Caribbean and Central America

GETTING TO KNOW THE BRITISH WEST INDIES
GETTING TO KNOW COSTA RICA, EL SALVADOR
     AND NICARAGUA
GETTING TO KNOW CUBA
GETTING TO KNOW GUATEMALA
     AND THE TWO HONDURAS
GETTING TO KNOW MEXICO
GETTING TO KNOW PANAMA
GETTING TO KNOW PUERTO RICO
GETTING TO KNOW THE VIRGIN ISLANDS

Europe; East and West

GETTING TO KNOW EASTERN EUROPE
GETTING TO KNOW ENGLAND, SCOTLAND, IRELAND
     AND WALES
GETTING TO KNOW FRANCE
GETTING TO KNOW GREECE
GETTING TO KNOW ITALY

GETTING TO KNOW POLAND
GETTING TO KNOW SCANDINAVIA
GETTING TO KNOW SPAIN
GETTING TO KNOW SWITZERLAND
GETTING TO KNOW THE SOVIET UNION
GETTING TO KNOW THE TWO GERMANYS

Middle East

GETTING TO KNOW IRAN-IRAQ
GETTING TO KNOW ISRAEL
GETTING TO KNOW LEBANON
GETTING TO KNOW SAUDI ARABIA
GETTING TO KNOW THE TIGRIS
     AND EUPHRATES RIVERS
GETTING TO KNOW TURKEY

North America

GETTING TO KNOW ALASKA
GETTING TO KNOW AMERICAN INDIANS TODAY
GETTING TO KNOW CANADA
GETTING TO KNOW THE MISSISSIPPI RIVER
GETTING TO KNOW THE U.S.A.

Pacific

GETTING TO KNOW AUSTRALIA
GETTING TO KNOW HAWAII
GETTING TO KNOW INDONESIA
GETTING TO KNOW MALAYSIA AND SINGAPORE
GETTING TO KNOW THE PHILIPPINES
GETTING TO KNOW THE SOUTH PACIFIC

South America

GETTING TO KNOW ARGENTINA
GETTING TO KNOW BRAZIL
GETTING TO KNOW CHILE
GETTING TO KNOW COLOMBIA
GETTING TO KNOW PERU
GETTING TO KNOW THE RIVER AMAZON
GETTING TO KNOW VENEZUELA

United Nations Agencies

GETTING TO KNOW F.A.O.
GETTING TO KNOW
     THE HUMAN RIGHTS COMMISSION
GETTING TO KNOW UNESCO
GETTING TO KNOW UNICEF
GETTING TO KNOW THE UNITED NATIONS
     PEACE FORCES
GETTING TO KNOW W H O
GETTING TO KNOW WMO